P9-DHP-273

Carol Lee,

Happiest of the big ones
Look up, heart in hand.
So many more to share—
Love, Father x
1995, December 15

Be an Angel

an alphabetical inspiration

Will Barker

Be an Angel

an alphabetical inspiration

Will Barker

Special thanks
to
family members and friends
whose advice
expertise
encouragement
and support
have made
this book a reality

∞

Will's dream come true

Copyright ©1992 Will Barker
All rights reserved.
No part of this book may be reproduced or transmitted in any form
or by any means, electronic, mechanical, photocopying, recording or
otherwise, without prior written permission from the publisher.
For information, contact Will's Works.

Will's Works
P.O. Box 5368
Eugene, Oregon 97405-9998
(541) 343-9325

Library of Congress Card Number: 95-90675

ISBN 0-9648718-0-7
10 9 8 7 6 5 4 3 2 1

Dedicated

to All

Present and Future

Angels

in

Loving Memory

of

Will

We
are all
Angels
when
our
hearts
are open

We
are all
Angels
when
our
hearts
are open

will barker © 92

Believe

in yourself

and miracles will happen

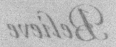

Believe
in yourself
and miracles will happen

will barker © 92

Care

for the divine spirit

in all things

Care

for the divine spirit

in all things

will barker © 92

Dream
without limits

Let
your
magic
wings
take flight

magic
wings
take flight

will barber © 92

Enjoy

simple

pleasures

Enjoy

simple

pleasures

will barker © 92

Free

your joy

until it fills

the skies

Free

your joy

until it fills

the skies

will barker © 92

Guide

with patience and kindness;

share the pathways you have found

Guide
with patience and kindness,
share the pathways you have found

will barker © 92

Help
whenever you can

We all need to be
taken care of sometimes

Help
whenever you can

*We all need to be
taken care of sometimes*

Invite

harmony

and

welcome

delight

Invite
harmony
and
welcome
delight

Join
together

Join
together

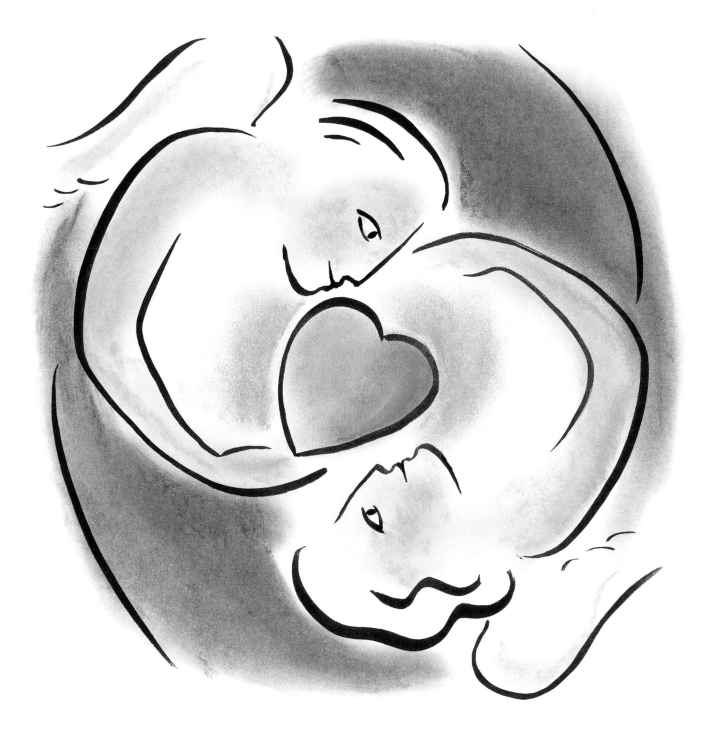

will barker © 92

Know
when to let go ...
Your love will follow

Know

... when to let go

Your love will follow

will barker © 92

Listen
to your heart

Listen
to your heart

will barker © 92

Mend
sorrow
with
tenderness

Mend

sorrow

with

tenderness

will barker © 92

*Nurture
friendships*

*A garden
can start
with just one rose*

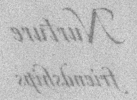

Nurture
Friendships

A garden
can start
with just one rose

will barker © 92

Offer

what

you

can

give

Offer
what
you
can
give

will barker © 92

Protect

your

ideals

Protect

your

ideals

Quiet
your mind

Leave time for angels
to pay a visit

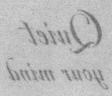

Quiet
your mind

Leave time for angels
to pay a visit

will barker © 92

Receive

the love

life brings

You deserve it

Receive

the love

life brings

You deserve it

will barker © 92

Support

another's hope

and your spirits will

kindle brighter

Support
another's hope
and your spirits will
kindle brighter

will barker © 92

Teach

your children well

Our thoughts

help shape

the world

Teach
your children well
Our thoughts
help shape
the world

will barker © 92

Untangle

Keep

it

simple

Untangle

Keep

it

simple.

will barker © 92

Value

innocence

Value

innocence

will barker © 92

Wing it

once in a while

Have faith

in your own courage

Wing it
once in a while
Have faith
in your own courage

will barker © 92

eXpress
yourself
You're alive!

eXpress
yourself

You're alive!

Yes!

you're

an

angel

will barker © 92

Take care
of
yourself
Even angels need their rest

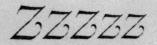

Take care
of
yourself
Even angels need their rest

will barker © 92

My work gives me pleasure. Sometimes it's fleeting, but occasionally, something — a line, a shape, a juxtaposition of colors — comes together in a way that's just right. It's those moments that keep me going.

March 17, 1954 – July 15, 1994

My work gives me pleasure. Sometimes it's fleeting, but occasionally, something – a line, a shape, a juxtaposition of colors – comes together in a way that's just right. It's those moments that keep me going.

March 17, 1954 – July 15, 1994

will barker © 92